DEBBIE RYAN

# BULLIED TO BROKEN

Copyright © 2020 by Debbie Ryan

A catalogue record for this book is available from the National Library of Australia

www.bkindco.com.au

Debbie Ryan (author)
Bullied to Broken: The true story of Maddy Ryan
ISBN 978-1-922337-79-5

Young Adult Nonfiction
Social Topics / Bullying
Social Topics / Suicide
Social Science / Psychology

Typeset Whitman 11/16

Cover and book design by Green Hill Publishing

in loving memory of
Maddy Ryan

# CONTENTS

# *Preface*

*Bullying is an ongoing misuse of power in relationships through repeated verbal, physical and/or social behaviour that causes physical and/or psychological harm. It can involve an individual or a group misusing their power over one or more persons. Bullying can happen in person or online, and it can be obvious (overt) or hidden (covert). Bullying of any form or for any reason can have long-term effects on those involved, including bystanders.*

Source: Bullying. NO WAY!

**THIS BOOK IS** Maddy's voice. This is a story of Maddy's journey through life and an account of her suffering from my perspective as her mother. Some of the information is verbatim from Maddy herself through her text messages, and accounts from those closest to her. This book records the decline of my daughter's mental health as a direct result of being bullied at a young age. It is my hope that this book shines a light for those being bullied, that they know that they are important, and that there is always help and support available. It is also a resource to assist others to support those who are being bullied, and give an insight into how bullying affects the individual. The story follows my journey through grief, and shows how love, resilience, positivity and strong networks can assist with life's challenges.

I hope that, at some level, this book will help to remove the stigma around mental health and to assist those who are suffering. It is a reminder to everyone to check on those they love, to ask questions and to monitor their own mental wellbeing. I have discovered that talking to those that care is the best therapy anyone can have.

My daughter, Maddy, suffered extreme bullying from a young age. The bullying lasted many years. This left her with psychological trauma, chronic self-esteem issues and anxiety, which she lived with daily. On 24 June 2018 Maddy took her own life, aged 23 years.

It was obvious to those who truly knew Maddy that she suffered from anxiety, although a mental health disorder was never diagnosed professionally. Maddy's anxiety at times was debilitating for her. Maddy suffered from regular heart palpitations, headaches, sleeplessness and stomach complaints. Often Maddy's emotional turmoil would leave her physically exhausted.

The people that were unkind to Maddy and made her suffer are not responsible for her death, but they were the catalyst for what became her mental health issues in life, her ongoing anxiety, fear and trust issues.

Maddy never wanted people to know her story. Maddy rarely had the strength to discuss the bullying at length, only to those she felt most comfortable with. I struggled with whether, or not, to tell Maddy's story. Was I dishonouring her wishes by telling her story? I honoured her wishes in life, I rarely spoke of what she went through and how hard life was for her, and our family at times. We are all part of a complex universe and we may think that our actions have no impact, but each action we take causes a ripple in the universe. We are all connected to each other. Maddy's story is also my story. I want our story to help others.

I am not a psychologist, I have no formal qualifications in this field – this is purely my personal journey in dealing with the effects of bullying and the subsequent death of my daughter. Ironically it is part of my corporate job to assist management in dealing with inappropriate workplace behaviour and harassment issues, but it is an entirely different experience dealing with the emotional damage bullying does to children, and particularly to my own child.

When clearing out some old documents after Maddy died, I came across the notes that I had made for the police when the bullying was at its worst. The police required a list, in a general sense, of various events and what happened to Maddy over the years. I had forgotten a lot, and found it confronting reading the notes again. One of Maddy's friends had kept every text message Maddy had ever sent to her from when they were young. I was given a copy of many of these messages and was further saddened reading how much she endured. After speaking with my son, he suggested I write a book about Maddy's story.

Bullying is a human rights issue. Bullying another individual is a violation of their human rights. It is imperative that schools, sporting clubs and workplaces ensure that they honour their duty of care and implement ongoing, evidence based programs to encourage healthy relationships. This duty of care is not only for physical wellbeing, but also for psychological wellbeing.

In a school environment, every teacher should complete a mental health first aid training course. In my opinion, identifying the signs of bullying is quite often half the battle, particularly when children are too scared to report incidents.

Children need to learn and develop appropriate social skills including empathy and respect for others. Children need to learn resilience, positivity and self-love among the negativity, and in many cases fake information, they are exposed to on social media.

My greatest wish is that people are kinder to each other.

# Acknowledgments

**SPECIAL THANKS TO** Sarah Quick for doing me the honour of writing the foreword for this book. I have great admiration for Sarah, for her professional success and her resilience in coping with the hurdles in her own life.

Special thanks to Paul Heywood-Smith QC for his expert legal advice during the construction of this book, and his personal support.

Thanks to those special people who have assisted me with editing this book, and for the valuable feedback I have received. Your feedback helped me in my determination to see this book published.

Special thanks must go to my son, Lochie; my rock in life, who encouraged me to write this book and not to give up.

Eternal thanks to Maddy for being my girl, for your kindness, love, strength and the lessons you taught me in life.

Part proceeds from the sale of this book will be donated to Breakthrough Mental Health Research Foundation to help fund mental health research.

# Foreword

*Kindly written by Sarah Quick, Assistant Commissioner for Victim's Rights, South Australia*

**AS A SOCIAL** worker and Assistant Commissioner for Victims' Rights I have spent most of my career witnessing the impact of trauma and seeking to assist those affected. In 2011, I undertook a project which saw me write an information booklet for people bereaved by suicide. When Debbie approached me to read her book I too was coming to terms with the loss of a loved one to suicide.

Based on my professional knowledge and personal experience, what I know for certain is that trauma has a devastating long-term impact and the effect of repeated trauma is cumulative. Debbie is determined, that by telling Maddy's story we may all understand the impact of trauma.

I like to imagine ourselves as mirrors, able to reflect the beauty around us. When we experience our first traumatic incident our mirror may fall and break into large pieces. But humans are resilient. We may be able to pick up those pieces, and stick them back in their place. We are still able to reflect the good in the world because despite a few cracks we are largely whole.

Each subsequent knock or trauma seems to break our mirror into smaller and smaller pieces. It becomes more and more difficult to find all the pieces and stick them in the correct places. The image we reflect becomes more and more fragmented. It also seems to take smaller and smaller knocks to dislodge all the pieces.

Some of us do not notice what is happening until faced with hundreds of tiny pieces on the ground. The task of putting them back together seemingly insurmountable.

The bullying Maddy endured is sickening. Contrary to what some may think Maddy was not weak, she was a strong individual whose confidence and self-worth were slowly eroded. In the end, her resilience was exhausted and she could no longer face the task of putting all her pieces back in place. This should never have happened.

This however, is not just Maddy's story, this is also Debbie's story, a powerful story of a mother's love, sorrow and determination. This is essentially a story for all of us including young people, parents and educators compelling us to do more to ensure no one else suffers as Maddy did.

It is Debbie's hope, and my own, that Maddy's story may cause us all to reflect on the impact of our behaviour towards others.

**- Sarah Quick**

# Introduction

**FOR THE BEST** part of a decade, during the time Maddy was bullied, I have wanted to do something to help stop bullying, but felt helpless in many ways during those years. There did not seem to be the support networks, media profile or resources to know how to help.

Several months after Maddy died I went to a conference organised by the South Australian Education Department. The conference was called "Keeping Children Safe from Bullying". There were over 900 people at this conference. It confirmed publicly, that bullying was a big problem for our community, and there were many people who wanted to stop bullying from occurring. I was relieved that the topic of bullying was out in the open, and being spoken about. There was discussion about punitive measures not being successful when dealing with children who bully. There was strong evidence that teaching children how to have healthy relationships had better outcomes.

The keynote speaker, Dr Wendy Craig is an international scientist and expert on bullying prevention. Dr Craig is the co-founder of a Canadian organisation called PREVNet (Promoting Relationships and Eliminating Violence Network). Dr Craig advocates working with scientific information and research to implement evidence-based policies in schools and other organisations where children are involved.

I found the information that was given at this conference challenging. As Maddy was a confident, happy, well-adjusted child prior to secondary school, I had surmised that Maddy's mental health issues stemmed from her bullying experiences. However, I did not fully understand the long-term impact it was going to have on her psychological wellbeing. I always hoped that she would get over the bullying experiences and live a happy life. Although the information on the psychological damage that bullying causes left me with sadness, it also gave me the determination to do something to help others in her name.

During the research for this book, I have read much about mental health issues. Although there are some genetic links to specific mental health disorders, there is a percentage of mental health issues that are created through environmental factors.

Bullying, teasing, victimization, relationship issues are considered environmental factors. We can change environmental factors. This gives me hope that as a community we can work together to make improvements for our children and future generations.

From the moment our children are born, there is an instinctive, overwhelming urge to protect them. As a mother, I have found that feeling has never left me even when my children became adults.

Being the mother of a daughter was not without its demands. I found myself in a constant quandary between loving her so much that I could burst and then flipping equally to annoyance when dealing with her occasional disrespect and anxiety-induced tantrums. Having said this, living through the ongoing harassment of my child by a small group of her peers, and not being able to protect her, seeing her slide into anxiety and despair at times – this was one of my greatest challenges in life.

If the community does not make a stand together; if people continue to sweep bullying under the carpet and not talk about it, if children are not taught how to have healthy relationships and accountability; and there is no ongoing education around this, nothing will change and the bullying scourge will continue.

The year Maddy died there were 3,046 deaths by suicide in Australia. These statistics were never reported publicly by the media. As much improvement, as there has been around mental health awareness there still appears to be a stigma attached to it. Perhaps the media could report more on the extent of the problem so that it stays paramount in conversation. The only way that we will stop the growing suicide rate is to understand what is causing it. Research into mental health is the key, and part of this is reporting on research data and statistics.

None of us is perfect, my daughter had her faults, but her good qualities far exceeded her faults. Maddy was kind-hearted, the sort of friend any of us would love to have, the sort of person that you would always feel comfortable telling your problems to, the sort of person who would do anything for anyone. So why would this type of person suffer from bullying? What made her a target? Both questions are equally elusive and difficult to answer. I can only make assumptions based on the information I was given by Maddy at the time.

I have had my own thoughts about why Maddy was bullied. My own opinion is that bullies seek weaker members of their group, those they can upset, this somehow makes them feel good about themselves. It always appeared to me that the key players had a desire for power, power over those that they perceived as having more than themselves.

In Maddy's case, Maddy was stunningly beautiful on the outside and equally beautiful on the inside. Maddy was an extremely sensitive and kind soul. Maddy loved animals and nature. Maddy was good at everything she put her mind to – playing the piano, sport, school, social activities – was it jealously? Was it that Maddy made the bullies feel inadequate at some level? Were they taking their own problems out on Maddy because they could, because they knew they could hurt her? I know Maddy would often ask me, "what do you think I did?", "why do you think they hate me?"

Perhaps the only people who could truly answer these questions are those people that bullied Maddy, but we did our best to keep them out of our lives and now it does not seem to have relevance for me. The fact is bullying happens, and as a community we should strive to stop it. We should do this for the sake of the mental health of future generations.

This book is a journey of a life taken too soon, the psychological trauma caused by bullying and unkindness, the repercussions of bullying on our family, our community, and the process of healing.

This is our story.

*Chapter 1*

# THE EARLY YEARS

**FROM MY EARLIEST** memories, I wanted to have a daughter. After several years of marriage, on the 17th January 1995 our beautiful daughter was born, Madeleine Paige Ryan weighing 7 pounds 10 ounces, healthy and utterly gorgeous. Both her father and I cried with happiness with her arrival – she was our greatest joy.

My little doll grew and grew, never cried unless she was hungry – she became more beautiful by the day, she was just such a happy child. Maddy's happiest times were playing in the garden with the dogs and chasing birds and butterflies. I didn't work for the first two and a half years of her life as I wanted to absorb every part of her development.

This was such a special time in my life. I just loved being a mother to her. We went shopping all the time with my mother, we were ladies that lunched a lot. Maddy was always in a hat or had a ribbon in her hair. I spent more money on her clothes and shoes than I did on my own.

Maddy loved people, especially other children and became close to her cousins, and many of my friends' children; they were her brothers and sisters in many respects. As they grew they shared many activities including birthdays and holidays. My friends and family would babysit her and Maddy became entrenched in these families as an integral part

of them. The relationships Maddy made with these children remained all her life. Even if time and circumstances separated them, whenever they caught up it was as though they had only seen each other yesterday. When Maddy died, these children, now adults were so affected, it was as though they had lost their own sister. With every door that closes, one opens. I have become closer with many of them, and I feel very blessed to have them in my life.

When I had to return to work part time, Maddy was two and a half years old. This was a difficult decision as I did not want to leave her, but it was time for me to go back to work.

I had met a woman and her child through our baby group which Maddy had been going to for a little over a year. This woman was just lovely and she was doing family day care from home. I felt comfortable leaving Maddy with her as I knew she had completed all the necessary checks. As the weeks progressed Maddy started to cry whenever I left her there. Maddy could not verbalise why, so one day I watched her interactions with the lady's daughter. The lady's daughter bossed Maddy around, would not let her play with the toys and Maddy was obviously sad and retreated to a corner of the room by herself. I told the lady that it was not working for us and I found an alternative arrangement for her.

Witnessing the interaction with Maddy and the little girl at the family day care was my first insight into Maddy's sensitivities if someone was mean to her. Maddy was just heartbroken whenever someone was cross with her, and it was obvious to me then that life was going to be cruel for her as some people can be mean; it is just part of life.

How was I going to protect her? These feelings of helplessness stayed with me. I tried to explain things to her but she was so young, she did not understand. Even as an adult, Maddy did not understand why people would be mean to her.

*Chapter 2*

# THE PRIMARY SCHOOL YEARS

**IN 2000 MADDY** commenced school. I was fearful for her. I wanted her happiness and personality to never be compromised, I never wanted her to know cruelty, I wanted to protect her, but I had to let her go.

I remember Maddy's first day of school so vividly. The sun was shining, she was so excited, she just wanted to go to school and make friends. I cried as she ran off waving at me, I was going to miss her being around. Maddy loved school and her friends, she was very happy.

Later that year, on 25th September 2000 Maddy's brother Lochie arrived. When Lochie arrived, Maddy was somewhat disappointed. Maddy desperately wanted a sister and asked me to send him back when she found out her new sibling was a boy. It didn't take long before Maddy took on her big sister duties with gusto, she loved taking care of him.

Maddy became very protective of her baby brother. Maddy liked to be involved in all aspects of his care, feeding and even changing the occasional nappy. Maddy was the best baby sitter, never letting him out of her sight.

Our family holidays were full of happiness and Maddy would always keep a watchful eye on her baby brother, I always felt he was safe when she was around.

Maddy had a wonderful learning experience at her primary school. Maddy's primary school was my old school, it was a Christian school with a beautiful community and wonderful staff. Maddy was popular, sporty and very happy. Her self-esteem was strong. Her primary school years were spent happy at school. Her family life was spent playing with animals, spending time with grandparents and extended family, close friends and she loved the beach. She was a happy, friendly child.

Facing the inevitable end of primary school, my husband and I spoke about what high school to send her to. We had discussed many options but decided on a private education as there were no well-reputed public schools in the area that we were zoned for.

Maddy had won a music scholarship playing piano in year seven. The scholarship was to a college near the city. Maddy did not want to leave her friends or her school, but understood that the scholarship would make it easier for us financially to send her to college.

The school strived for good academic results, and I knew, not long into the first term, that Maddy was not coping with the academic pressure. The school also put extra pressure on Maddy to play another instrument. The school suggested the cello. Maddy practiced piano and cello diligently. Over the following months of the first term I noticed that Maddy was losing weight. I went through Maddy's bag and found several weeks' worth of rotting food at the bottom of her backpack. When I spoke to Maddy about this she started to cry. Maddy said that she was struggling with the academic pressure, she missed her friends and wanted to go back to her primary school to finish year 7. Seeing her distress, I agreed and Maddy returned to her local primary school to finish her primary school years.

Maddy was much happier, although I did suspect that she had lost confidence because her experience in a new school had not worked out. Some of her friendships became strained as a result. Primary school came to its inevitable end and Maddy graduated with many celebrations.

My memories of the graduation party were of a night filled with noise and excitement. The children celebrating the end of an era, the end of that chapter of their lives. Maddy looked beautiful, we had her hair done and she had a new dress. There were groups of children laughing and chatting.

I remember Maddy playing with a blue balloon. Maddy did not participate much in the group chatter, she did not carry on with much of the excitement of the party. Instead, for whatever reason, she played with the balloon – throwing it in the air, catching it, chasing it if it escaped – she had a smile on her face and she looked content. I looked at her and it reminded me of when she was little, chasing the butterflies and the birds.

My own opinion is that she was happy that she graduated with her friends from the school she loved. I believe she was just enjoying the experience, the experience of being a child and not thinking about what the future held.

*Chapter 3*

# THE SECONDARY YEARS

**ULTIMATELY MADDY CHOSE** the high school she was to attend. Many of Maddy's friends were going to the school and Maddy looked forward to the new beginning of her high school years. The school was local and had a good reputation among those that were in our network.

From the first week, my daughter had joined a large group of boys and girls. These children were thought of as the popular group. Many of these children were sporty and were popular with each other, or so it seemed.

As time went by during that first year, we noticed a change in Maddy's behaviour. Maddy became withdrawn, not talking very much and would often cry. Maddy complained of stomach pain and headaches, anything she could think of to stay home. Several of the female members of the group had started being mean to her. In many cases it was just subtle exclusion, and I put it down to school yard nonsense and childish behaviour. I hoped it would pass.

I offered Maddy as much emotional support as I could and we crossed one hurdle at a time. It did appear from an outside perspective that this group of children knew they could get to her, that they could make her cry. Maddy told me that she would often stay in the bathroom all lunch time to avoid them.

The dynamics of this group were complex. There did not appear to be one leader, it appeared to fluctuate. There seemed to be more issues with a couple of them, particularly those with the stronger personalities. There were boys and girls in this group and often power struggles appeared within the group causing conflict among some of them.

There was not a defining incident that started the bullying that I recall. Information obtained from her friends, was that Maddy became an easy target. I was advised that the group of children who bullied Maddy would often talk about her behind her back. According to Maddy, there were apparently untrue rumours started about her and nasty things said over social media. Often Maddy would be distressed that they had left her out of group chats. Maddy would become scared and upset about what they were saying about her, and what the other children thought of her. This was the time her fear of rejection appeared. This fear stayed with her all her life and influenced many of her relationships.

I was told by one of Maddy's friends that the early bullying events were mainly exclusion. As well as being excluded on social media, Maddy was not invited to sleep overs and was excluded in the school yard. One of Maddy's friends told me that Maddy would often run off crying. This young woman advised me after Maddy died, that she would often see self-harm marks on Maddy's arms and legs, and that Maddy always kept them covered. I realised she was harming herself in the later years, but was unaware that it started so early. I often think, how did I miss this? I am not even sure I knew what self-harm was 10 years ago or what caused it. Looking back, I was naive about mental health and the effects bullying had on my daughter. I completely underestimated the intense pain that people's unkindness caused her.

*When children are involved in bullying as aggressors, they are experiencing regular lessons in the use of power and aggression to control and distress others. Children who are victimized become trapped in a disrespectful relationship in which they become increasingly powerless*

I remember one incident where Maddy had told me that she looked at a mobile phone that belonged to one of the girls in the group. Maddy told me she felt guilty about looking at the girl's phone, but wanted to know what the group were saying about her. One of Maddy's friends sent me a phone message after she died about the same incident. Maddy said that there were so many lies in the messages about her, it traumatised her to think others believed what the group were saying. It also upset her immensely that the girl whose phone she looked at said that she was Maddy's friend, but participated in the group chats that were fuelling lies about Maddy. Maddy could never understand why people that called themselves her friends would stay in contact with the group that caused her so much pain.

One of Maddy's text messages said "I know all the girls were invited. X posted it in the group message. I was the only girl not invited."

Another incident that caused Maddy distress was when the group "unfriended" her on social media. It appeared to me to be a punishment. They eventually followed her again, but it just seemed cruel to me to do that to her. The girls would often be nice to Maddy, gain her trust and then there would be a drama and Maddy would be wounded again.

Maddy refused to tell me much of what was said to her. By the end of the first year, Maddy was suffering with obvious self-esteem issues. Maddy's self-talk became negative as time went on. "I am a terrible person that is why they don't like me" or "I am useless". These phrases I heard a lot over the following years. Maddy said to me that she did not belong anywhere, she did not fit in and she had nothing to offer.

A message from Maddy stated, "They hate me I don't even know what I've ever done to them, they are just horrible."

I noticed Maddy's personality was changing, she was rarely happy and would get angry, having outbursts over the most trivial things. I knew the bullying was affecting her but I thought perhaps she was just being over sensitive and that it would all blow over.

By her second year of high school the bullying events seemed to escalate. The harassment did appear to be more constant. I started getting the school involved, as I could see how the bullying was hurting her. Maddy cried a lot, she was lonely, she started to withdraw more frequently from our family, and fun events in our life. Maddy would say "Mum it is dark and lonely where I am", "I don't want to be here, life is too hard". I remember the first time she said that to me, it cut through my heart like a knife. I adored both of my children, I loved them more than I thought imaginable, I gave them everything I possibly could, I continued working part time so I could be there for them, I did everything within my power to help my children. How could Maddy feel this way when she was so loved? To get Maddy back to a good place took many conversations and support, and the stress I felt during these times was intense.

*Social media often left Maddy feeling like she was not good enough*

Much of the harassment Maddy received was over Facebook and text messages. It appeared to me that the bullies seemed to have increased courage when they could hide behind technology.

Social media can have such a detrimental influence on our children, and many adults. People are subtly convinced about how they should look, what clothes they should buy and what a perfect life looks like. If they cannot achieve these things, often it puts them under pressure, and makes them feel inadequate. Many people posting information over social media only ever post what they want us to see; the good parts of their lives. Much

of what is posted is embellished and enhanced. People rarely show what their reality truly is. Social media provides the opportunity for people to comment and make judgment on the lives of others. Social media often left Maddy feeling like she was not good enough, not thin enough, not smart enough and it left her with a false impression of what a perfect life was supposed to look like.

Maddy did not have a mobile phone until high school but as I was working longer hours I needed to be in touch with her. Maddy was very happy when she received her first mobile phone. However, once the bullying presented, cyberbullying became a real issue for Maddy and that appeared to be an avenue for the bullies to get to her over the years. Maddy was never free from the bullying when it was at its worst. I would often walk past her bedroom door and hear her crying. Technology allowed these people into our home, into her bedroom, her safe places; there was no escaping them. Many teenagers use technology to stay in touch, to feel connected to each other. For Maddy, technology exacerbated her pain and left her feeling lonely and isolated from others. The result of this was that she often lived with feelings of fear - fear of not being liked, fear of rejection, fear of having no friends, fear of what the bullies were saying about her and fear of what others thought of her.

The isolation that social media left Maddy with was cruel. I remember often sitting on her bed chatting about how she could feel so isolated and lonely when there were so many people who loved her. In the later years Maddy seemed to be so popular and have so many people in her life. It has since become obvious to me that Maddy's feelings of loneliness were residual from her early years where she was isolated from her group of friends. Humans are social beings and therefore need to feel like they fit into their group. I believe this makes people feel valued, with a sense of belonging.

*Loneliness is a feeling of sadness or distress about being by yourself or feeling disconnected from the world around you. It may be felt*

I believe that if the people you have in your life do not make you feel valued, you should find other people to spend your time with. For some reason, Maddy always sought the approval of the group that hurt her, and it became a pattern in her life that her whole self-worth was determined by how they were treating her on any given day. As the years passed, this self-worth was determined by how others treated her. Maddy could never find her own self-worth or believe in it.

Through Maddy's life she would become wounded when she would see people on social media, who said they were her friends, having happy snaps with the people that bullied her. I would say to Maddy that people have a right to be friends with whomever they like, but you have the power to control what you see on social media. Even though Maddy saw it as betrayal and lack of consideration on their part, she always wanted to see what others were doing even if it upset her.

It was not until I saw one of her friends with the group that bullied Maddy pop up on social media recently, that I felt Maddy's pain. Did this young woman not realise that she had requested me to follow her, did she think I would not care, did she not care? These were all questions that I was left with. I did not want that reminder, so I did something that Maddy could never do, I stopped following her. There is a lesson for everyone here. If something you see on social media upsets you and makes you feel uncomfortable, get it out of your life. It is very empowering to have control over what you are seeing visually and letting into your life. This is particularly true for social media. Life and everything in it should be uplifting for you.

> Maddy stated, "I feel like shit every day of my life because of them."

I would say that Maddy was like a puppy who got kicked, she would always go back wagging her tail with forgiveness in her heart. A message from Maddy stated, "I feel like shit every day of my life because of them."

Maddy was easy to hurt. Maddy was sensitive and giving. Maddy always put others before herself. The people who hurt her during her life, not only the bullies, but those who were supposed to love and care for her contributed to her suffering in life by treating her without sensitivity and kindness. None of these people are absolved from contributing to her mental health decline. If people were kinder to Maddy, I believe we would still have her with us.

As life progressed for Maddy, and she began different relationships, inevitably her anxiety and fear would fracture many of those relationships. Over time Maddy truly believed that it was all her fault that things would go pear shaped in her relationships, that there was something wrong with her. Some of the people she became involved with were just horrible. I would say to her that she picked the wrong people to socialise with and that is why she got hurt. It was not her, but her choices in company that needed to change. I often reminded her that she always deserved better, but she never believed me.

Some of the issues at school seemed trivial, but at the time they were very important to Maddy and perpetuated her self-loathing. This often affected our family life severely. Maddy would get angry and had trouble at times controlling this. Her pain had to come out somehow. Some of the things she said to me over the years were cruel and left me feeling like I had failed her. I had a constant feeling of sickness at the thought of people being mean to her, that the wider group was also excluding her. I hated the thought that she was sitting in the bathroom on a toilet seat, all alone, eating her lunch. I felt helpless at these times.

One day Maddy told me another girl came into the bathroom with her lunch as she was trying to avoid the same people. Maddy said that this made her feel better, that it was not just her that they were picking on. This young lady and Maddy became life-long friends, and she was there for Maddy until the end. At each incident with the bullies, when Maddy would go into despair, I would contact the school again.

Knowing how sensitive Maddy was, I remember very distinctly having a conversation about bullying policies with the school before Maddy started. The school hierarchy assured me that the school was hot on it and there was a bullying policy accessible to all students and parents. As it turned out this was a tiny diagram in the front of the school diary. There was no significant policy that I was ever referred to.

With each complaint, the school hierarchy would say all the right things about how they would support Maddy. They tried to offer solutions but as Maddy was too scared to ever formally complain, I felt at the time that this gave the school a way out, not to investigate things further. From my perspective, there appeared to be no effective support, mediation, or programs to help the children to understand the impact of bullying, or build healthy relationships. My husband and I, and especially Maddy, felt alone and unsupported by the school during those high school years.

I believe that the school teaching community could have made a positive impact in Maddy's life during those years. More could have been done to intervene and help prevent the bullying and harassment that Maddy endured. Maddy told me that there were no teachers that she felt comfortable approaching to discuss the bullying. Maddy felt that nobody cared. Perhaps the incidents were not discussed with the wider teaching community, maybe they were not aware of what was happening. Perhaps they did not have the skills to identify that Maddy was struggling.

On one occasion one of the bullies threatened, on Facebook, to harm Maddy if she came back to school. It was early in the morning and she was getting ready for school. I could hear Maddy sobbing. Maddy was curled up in a ball on the floor, half naked, crying hysterically saying that this girl threatened to hurt her if she returned to school. I tried to settle her down, I held her, I said I would try to fix it. I contacted the school and was advised that they could access the children's Facebook pages and get the police involved if I wanted to go that far. I had to consult with Maddy and do what she felt comfortable with. Unfortunately, Maddy was too afraid of the consequences and would not pursue it. Maddy was 14 at the time, this was too much for her to process. In my corporate position, if an incident is reported, we have a duty of care for all staff to investigate that report whether, or not, the victim wants to make a formal complaint. I believe the school should have done more to investigate the reports.

I often said to Maddy that I would close her social media so that she would not be hurt anymore. Maddy would say that if I closed her social media this would isolate her even more from her peers. I would often confiscate her mobile phone overnight just so she would get a decent night's sleep. Maddy always wanted to know what they were saying to others about her. As a parent, these decisions are difficult at the time, and you do not want to cause the child additional distress.

I had offered on several occasions to remove Maddy from the school but she said that bullying would happen to her wherever she went to school as she was "just one of those people that others don't like." After two years of constant bullying her self-esteem was shattered and she had very little self-confidence. I feared that change of any kind would not help her at that point.

My paramount concern was for my daughter's emotional health. We had suffered the loss of my father, whom she was very close to. We all felt emotionally fragile at that time, and I did not want to make things any worse for any of us so I decided not to remove her from the school.

I look back at the choices I made at the time and think, what if I had removed her from school, would it have made a difference? Would she have recovered and led a happier life? The truth is I really do not know. None of us would intentionally make a bad decision, we can only make our decisions based on the circumstances and information we have at that moment.

The trauma seemed to be so deep within Maddy at that stage. My priority was trying to make her happy and give her as stress-free a life as I could. I have arrived at the conclusion, since Maddy died, that hindsight is a pointless concept. I cannot go back and change anything, so why waste energy wondering what I could have done differently? The fact is that my priority was always Maddy, every decision I made was because I thought it was the best one for her at the time, and each of those decisions came from a place of love.

By Maddy's third year of high school in 2010 she had started going out with one of the boys in her group. Initially this was fine for her. We became fond of him and he appeared to be a good support for her. She adored him and in many ways, he was her rock during her difficult times that year.

Maddy went back to her primary school to do work experience. Maddy was an excellent netball player. Maddy's sports teacher from primary school worked with Maddy during this week and encouraged Maddy to pursue teaching. The teacher said that Maddy was a natural with children, and she could see how the children were drawn to her. This teacher was Maddy's champion during this time giving her a part-time job coaching the junior netball team. Maddy loved working in her old school with the children, and continued with her coaching and umpiring until she left school. Having employment was good for Maddy, she always worked hard and tried to do her best. Work helped her to feel better about herself and seemed to help with her anxiety as it kept her busy, with less time to think.

During that year there were more parties and socialising outside of school. I do remember Maddy telling me that there was an altercation between her and the girls at one of the parties. The weeks that followed were so very stressful.

*Maddy would not get out of bed, let alone go to school.*

One of the bullies sent Maddy a barrage of insulting text messages over something Maddy said she did not do. Maddy said that she did not understand why this girl was so angry with her. None of the other girls would speak to her and shut her out of their group for some time. They did this by not speaking to her in the school yard, not responding to any of her Facebook communication, and not responding to telephone calls. This sent Maddy into a spiral of despair. Maddy would not get out of bed, let alone go to school. I called my manager at the time in tears to explain what was happening to her, I had to take days off work to support her through this period. I was very worried about her mental health during this time.

I knew that Maddy was in a severe emotional state. I did not want to make waves or make things worse for her. I did not think that she would cope with it. Instead I thought long and hard about a strategy of dealing with what I faced as her mother.

I contacted the school. I told them exactly what had happened. I told them I did not want my daughter to go through the public trauma of having the group know that I had contacted the school. Instead I asked that the school address the children as a group and talk about bullying and the effects that it had on those who are victimised. The school did as I asked.

For a very short time, this seemed to work, it obviously struck a chord with those who had a guilty conscience. However, by this time Maddy was really struggling and was miserable going to school. Maddy's self-esteem was at rock bottom.

It was Maddy's opinion that there were two key players in the group that bullied Maddy. They were female. According to Maddy, she believed these two girls were the instigators of the bullying. Many of the other children participated by excluding Maddy whenever issues arose. Maddy did not feel supported by the wider group. Maddy often felt hurt by the others in the group because they did not help her. They conformed to whatever the two key bullies implemented. This perpetuated her feelings of inadequacy and loneliness.

Many of the people in Maddy's peer group, boys and girls, in effect, supported the bullying behaviour by not intervening when Maddy was being harassed by the main culprits. I have discovered that many of Maddy's peers knew she was struggling, but did not help her. They chose to leave her alone which perpetuated her self-hatred. These people added to Maddy's pain. Their lack of intervention does not excuse them from the part they played in her suffering. Sometimes witnessing bullying events can be traumatic, but bystanders can help the victim by confidentially reporting inappropriate behaviour to authorities.

Statistics reported on Stomp Out Bullying state that "when someone stands up to bullying, 57% of the time the bullying stops within 10 seconds." Our society needs to encourage heroes for those being bullied in school yards, work places and sporting organisations. People who report incidents should feel supported, and I believe this would encourage more open communication around bullying.

There were a couple of girls that had the courage to leave the group. As a result, they were ridiculed and heckled regularly by the bullies, according to Maddy. On one occasion, I remember Maddy coming home and saying that she had sat with these two girls at lunch time. Because of that, Maddy was then being harassed by the bullies telling her to "come back from the dark side". Maddy felt bad for the girls. Maddy said to me that it had taken the attention away from her, and that was a relief. Maddy said that she would not have enough courage to leave the group, as she would not want to go through any further harassment.

In her fourth year of high school, conflict was starting to appear between Maddy and her boyfriend. Their relationship became volatile. This compounded Maddy's lack of self-esteem. Maddy was continually on a roller coaster ride with the bullies. From one day to the next she did not know whether they would include her or exclude her. Maddy and her boyfriend were young and both not equipped to deal with her anxiety, which was very evident by this stage. Maddy said she wanted her life to end – she said she found nothing in life worth living for.

I remember being shocked when she said this to me. I thought to myself - how can life be that bad that you could feel this way? Can you imagine the pain of hearing your child say that they could not find anything in life worth living for? Can you imagine the feelings I had toward this group of bullies who were causing her pain and harassing her?

I remember saying to Maddy at our lowest point "please tell me what I can do to help you?" I will always remember her reply "just find me a friend". I cannot even describe how much these words hurt me as her mother. I felt helpless and in despair myself. As a result, I contacted a girl in her year level who I knew I could trust. I met her after school and told her what had been happening. I sobbed as I recounted Maddy's troubles. This beautiful girl was very aware of what Maddy had been going through. She became Maddy's angel and watched over her.

After Maddy died, I found beautiful letters from this girl that Maddy had kept. Maddy had a treasure box of letters and cards that spoke positively and kindly to her. Although it was nice to know how many people loved her, it made me sad at the time that Maddy could not hold those thoughts and people in her mind, and feel better about herself.

I also discovered, after Maddy's death, that this beautiful girlfriend of Maddy's had taken her to the doctor to see if there was something he could do for her. I never knew this, Maddy never told me. Maddy was referred to a psychologist, but her friend told me she refused to go.

Maddy suffered from fear of what people thought of her. Maddy believed that if people found out she had mental health issues that she would be judged, and it would be another reason people had for not wanting to be around her. I suggested Maddy seek professional help on more than one occasion, but she would always refuse. Maddy often told me that she did not need professional help, that I was enough for her, that my advice helped her to see clearly. I was not equipped for this, I was not educated in such matters, but I read as many books as I could to help me to help her. I often felt such a burden that I was the one that she relied on, at times it scared me. Not a burden in the sense of being the one she always went to, but a burden in that I did not have the necessary knowledge to help her.

Most days my phone would ping with text messages. If Maddy was struggling those pings would be constant, sometimes up to 20 a day at her most troubled times. Quite often lengthy text messages too. I just kept fighting alongside her, trying to offer encouragement and trying to get her to believe a different truth about herself. I continue to miss those text messages.

Maddy never felt comfortable around strangers, and talking to a psychologist who was a stranger to her, about her deepest and darkest fears, was something Maddy always flatly refused to participate in.

I did take Maddy to our family doctor to see if he could help her. He suggested that she also see a psychologist to help her with strategies on how to cope. Maddy again refused. Our family doctor was a wonderful man who I felt comfortable with, and someone that I went to see when issues arose that were particularly difficult for me to manage.

As my daughter would not seek professional help I researched natural ways to help her. I spoke to a naturopath and she suggested magnesium. I bought some magnesium powder and made her fruit smoothies with it every morning. I do believe this helped her. Before bedtime, when she was particularly stressed, she would take a Valerian capsule, which is a natural herb, to help her sleep. Sometimes I would lay in bed with her so that I could feel close to her and hoped that it helped her to feel like she was not alone, that someone loved her.

I often said to her, I love you enough for 100 people, I love you more than life itself, surely my love is enough for you. It never seemed to be, she always sought the approval of others.

I had read an article about how animals can help people with mental health issues. Animals are a great leveller, they love unconditionally, they know when you are sad and they enjoy life no matter what!

I decided to buy Maddy a Pug puppy. This was the beginning of our love affair with the breed. When Maddy first met Lola, it was love at first sight, I will never forget the look on Maddy's face. Lola slept with Maddy, Lola became her best friend, Lola made her happy, which was something I had not seen a lot of through her secondary school years.

Consequently, whenever life got desperate for Maddy, I would buy another Pug. We currently have three of the little darlings. They did give her a lot of joy, and now, no matter how crazy our life is with the three of them running around, I remain grateful to their little souls for the happiness they gave her.

By Maddy's final year things were slightly easier for her at school. Maddy could come and go more freely because of her class timetable.

Maddy remained with her boyfriend and they went to their school formal together that year. Maddy looked beautiful, and they had a wonderful night. I was so pleased this was a good experience for her.

The exclusion and harassment did continue periodically that year. One incident I do recall was "Schoolies". Schoolies is the end of year school celebration held over a long weekend. I remember her calling me to ask whether I could book a tent site for her and the girls as they were not having any luck securing a site.

I felt uneasy about this as I knew there were still ongoing issues between her and the girls. Maddy said that if she helped the girls, maybe things would be better between all of them. I was concerned that she was safe and protected while she was at Schoolies so I called the caravan park to ask what services they provided for the teenagers attending. They assured me that there was a lot of security and people watching them so I felt better that there were people that she could go to if she needed.

I went ahead and booked the site for the girls. As we had organised it and I had to pay, Maddy coordinated the collection of all the money from the girls. There were approximately ten of them so this was not a stress-free task, but Maddy collected the money and I sent off the cheque to the caravan park where they were staying.

A couple of weeks before Schoolies, Maddy came home from school crying and distressed. Maddy advised me that most of the girls were staying in one big tent and there were a couple of them that were told they would have to organise another tent on the outer perimeter of the site. My husband was furious, and wanted to cancel the site. He felt that the girls were again bullying the others by not including them, and Maddy was the one who had organised everything. I spoke to Maddy and the other girls about it and they seemed fine, at least they had each other so I relaxed about it, at least temporarily.

I followed them in my car to the site and helped the girls erect their tent. I was worried about the bullying and Maddy being around the group. There were no other parents there. Only one of the girls from the other group came up to me to say hello. The remainder of the girls watched me helping the girls erect their tent - not one of them acknowledged me. These girls had been to my house for sleepovers, I had cooked for them, I had been kind to them, for those reasons alone I would have expected them to acknowledge me, to say hello, to show respect – each of them ignored me completely. In fact, I purposely tried to make eye contact with the main bullies during the time I was there. I wanted them to look me in the eyes, and for them to know that I was aware of what they were doing to Maddy. Each of them avoided my gaze; they looked at the ground or looked the other way. I was furious.

As I was helping the girls unpack and get settled, Maddy and I glanced at each other, the pain and hurt on her face cut through me like someone had kicked me in the stomach with such ferocity that it had halted my breath. I wanted to turn around and take her home with me. I told her to call me straight away if it got too much for her or the other girls.

All I could see was the hurt on Maddy's face as I left in my car. I was so stressed about leaving her there, I cried. I called a girlfriend who did not live far just so I had someone to talk to. I told my girlfriend, who knew the history of bullying Maddy had experienced, how I felt. I told her that there were periods over the last 5 years where I thought my daughter was dramatizing, that it could not possibly be as bad as what she said. Maddy would often tell me that she felt invisible. After experiencing it first hand, I realized that there was truth in everything she had said, as I had been made to feel invisible too. I had a mixture of emotions, sickness, guilt, anger – but most of all admiration for this seventeen year old girl who could find the strength to rise above it all.

> *I finally realised that each of the bullying events that Maddy had complained about were real, and not just an overreaction on her part.*

This incident was a defining moment for me. I finally realised that each of the bullying events that Maddy had complained about were real, and not just an overreaction on her part. I was confronted with the horrible realisation that I had completely underestimated the deep and hurtful impact Maddy's peer group had on her, and the deep psychological scars that she was left with. I look back now and wonder how I could possibly have been so naïve about how deeply these people hurt her.

To this day I am in awe of how Maddy got through those years, all that she endured from the group, the troubled, toxic relationship she had with her boyfriend, and the lack of support she received from her school. Maddy showed a great resilience to bounce back from each of these events in her life.

Since Maddy's death, there have been people that have said to me that she was weak to take her own life. If people truly knew Maddy's suffering, the psychological trauma that she endured, the anxiety that she lived with and the strength it took to face these people day in and day out; Maddy is one of the strongest people I have ever known. I would like to encourage people to never judge someone when you cannot possibly know their experiences or situation in life.

Maddy's school is a beautiful school, with a good teaching community, however, I continue to be disappointed in the inadequacy of appropriate behaviour policies and the lack of investigation into the incidents that I had reported. I do understand that bullying did not have as high a profile all those years ago, but from a duty of care perspective and consideration for student wellbeing, in my opinion, the school hierarchy were not there for Maddy.

Schools need to take responsibility for what goes on in their grounds, and in their classrooms. Any whisper of bullying needs to be taken seriously, and acted upon immediately. Programs should start in the early years where healthy relationships are encouraged and created.

Just because a child is too scared to complain, does not mean the bullying does not exist. Investigate the truth and help all students to have relationships with each other that are kind and empathetic. Children have a right to feel safe and protected.

People have asked me what the parents of these children were like. They seemed like nice people. At one stage, I did approach one of the mothers and said that Maddy was suffering from bullying. The woman said to me "that is just what girls do." As the years passed and they grew into adulthood, I read a message from Maddy that said the daughter of this woman had tried to push her over in a night club. Given the response from the young woman's mother, I came to believe that these girls were overindulged and were not held accountable for their actions in life.

High school ended. I remember her last day as clearly as anything. Maddy held her head high, participated in everything that everyone else did. All the time I watched her, and them, to make sure her experience was not tarnished. I watched her in amazement, hide her pain and participate with laughter in the soap and water antics of their final break up.

Maddy's beautiful girlfriend had a bad injury that had led to chronic pain. This saw her receive unkind treatment, also from the group of teenagers that called themselves her friends. I remember Maddy worrying about her not being able to participate.

Due to her injury, Maddy's girlfriend was sitting alone on the side of the lawn, watching all the year twelves mess about, and she was crying. I just wanted to hug her but did not want to make a scene. Out of nowhere Maddy rushed up to her, covered in soap suds, and hugged her so hard that she was also covered in suds. I snapped a photograph of this moment. The look on both of their faces was priceless. That showed me that Maddy's essence was still there, what made her good and kind, that child that I had raised, the one that was happy with the simple things in life, she was still in there. Maddy's kindness and compassion was not something they could take away from her.

When she came home there was such an outpouring of tears. Maddy sobbed. I was so worried, but she said that it was relief, and not to worry. Maddy said it was all over, but unfortunately it was not.

*Chapter 4*

# POST SCHOOL YEARS

**SCHOOL LIFE ENDED** and Maddy found herself alone. The group appeared to drop her like a hot potato. There were a couple of girls who kept in contact with her and she focused on building those friendships. Those friends were close to Maddy for the remainder of her life.

Maddy spent five years trying to get her group to like her and treat her as they did most of the others. It did not seem to matter how much I begged her to drop the lot of them, she always had faith that she could see good in them, and that things would get better for her.

Maddy's end of school results came through and Maddy achieved a better than expected ATAR. This astonished me. How Maddy could get through any of her schoolwork with all that was going on was a miracle. This showed me how hard Maddy worked to be as good as she could be. It was during these years Maddy developed her perfectionist nature. Maddy had a huge drive for perfectionism in all aspects of her life. In Maddy's mind, this gave the bullies less to pick on. Maddy confessed this to me on more than one occasion. I believe this gave them more ammunition to hurt her. It appeared to me

> *It appeared to me that the more Maddy achieved, the more the bullies would pick on her.*

that the more Maddy achieved, the more the bullies would pick on her. This in turn would make Maddy put more pressure on herself to be perfect. Failure was never acceptable to her. Maddy got into her first university preference and was set for her new start.

There was a lovely group of young people from her school that I had been encouraging Maddy to become friends with for years, but Maddy never had the courage to leave the group that made her life a misery. Maddy saw how the bullies treated people who left the group and never wanted to face their wrath. However, due to the exclusion by the other group, it made it easier for me to convince Maddy to pursue closer friendships with the nice group of young adults. During that year she became friends with them and found happiness with her new group.

Until Maddy's death, these friends rallied around her, they made her feel special, they understood her anxiety and where it came from, they included her and valued her. The only time Maddy saw the bullies were at parties of mutual friends, and at night clubs. Maddy often came home and said that bottles had been thrown at her. I always worried for her safety at these times.

The same exclusion Maddy felt at school would often happen in the night clubs. Unfortunately, with alcohol in the mix things often escalated. On one occasion, her boyfriend had to stand between her and two of the bullies to prevent Maddy being physically injured.

One of Maddy's text messages stated, "X and X were pushing me again lol and X (Maddy's boyfriend) was getting so angry and just swung me around and started pushing them back."

After this event, where Maddy felt physically threatened, she came home and said that she did not want to have anything more to do with that group. The relief I felt at her decision was immense.

During this time, Maddy also ended her relationship with her boyfriend. Over the years, the relationship had become volatile and toxic and all of those around her knew she should end it. Once upon a time, Maddy would never have considered this, she would often stress just at the thought of not being with him. I felt that she had developed strength to know what she wanted in life, and that had to be a good thing.

Unfortunately, it was within a very short time of her ending her relationship with her boyfriend that Maddy found out that he had gone off with one of the young women in the group of bullies. According to the text message that Maddy sent, this young woman was one of the women who had tried to push her over in the night club, one that had been so horrible to her.

The devastation this caused Maddy, set her back emotionally. Maddy felt so betrayed and this life event was one of the most monumental sufferings in her life. From that time, all relationships she had - endured her lack of trust and suspicion. Maddy became physically ill with stomach complaints, heart palpitations and headaches for some time. I would hear her crying at night. Maddy said that life hurt too much and she did not want to feel the pain anymore.

I have always been one to treat people as they treat me, I could not hate her boyfriend as he had always been kind to me. I did not like the way he treated Maddy, but hate was not something I felt for anyone, Maddy and I argued over this on more than one occasion. Having said that, I also felt the betrayal that out of all the girls he could have gone out with, he picked one from the group that had been involved in bullying and excluding her for all those years. I did let him know of my disappointment in him, of the way he treated her and I did close off communication with him after this.

After rejecting a birthday invitation for one of the girls it came out that Maddy did not want to be around the group anymore. Over the next few weeks, my daughter received, what seemed to be endless harassment and extreme bullying. To say that this made her life miserable would be an understatement, in fact, I have no words to adequately explain the pain that they caused her and our family during this time.

There was a man who had sent Maddy a filthy message on Facebook. She deleted him immediately. He called her and asked why she had deleted him as a friend. Maddy advised that she did not want to be spoken to in such a filthy way, she was utterly disgusted. He replied that she was talking filthy words to him on the phone, so he thought it was OK. He said that when she allegedly called she was with one of the girls in the group. Maddy replied that she was no longer friends with that girl, and that she had never spoken to him. He apologised. I was very worried over this event. If the young man had not bothered to contact her, he could have gone about tarnishing her reputation for something she had nothing to do with. Or worse, he could have met up with her unwittingly and called in the sexual promises. I knew there had to be some criminal charges we could investigate over this incident. I wanted to contact the police but Maddy would not let me. As Maddy was now 18 and was an adult I had lost control over how much I could pursue on her behalf.

Within a few days, a harassing text message was sent to her from another member of the group accusing her of something she did not do. The next day our house had eggs thrown at it during the night. There was a concentration of egg around my daughter's window. The eggs were rotten and stunk, they stuck to our beautiful home, our haven, like glue, a visual reminder to Maddy of how much they hated her. Maddy's despair and anxiety was extreme after our house was egged.

By this stage, I was beyond anger, I was so distressed, I felt constantly sick. To add to my own distress, I had to consider Maddy. Maddy said that she felt guilt that this had happened to our house. Guilt that their hate for her had upset me. I tried to assure Maddy that it was not her, that it said more about them, but she did not hear my words. As our house had been vandalised, I immediately contacted the police and told them about the egging. They asked if Maddy had any recent issues with bullying. I advised that my daughter had been harassed and bullied for many years at school; personally, and over Facebook and text messages. I explained the issues and the range of bullying behaviour, including the filthy telephone conversation where someone pretended to be Maddy.

The policeman took the details. I advised him that we had text message evidence of much of the bullying as Maddy had not deleted the messages. I gave the policeman the names of each of the young women in the group of bullies that I suspected could have been involved. The policeman said that he would investigate the people that had been harassing Maddy. We discussed options about restraining orders and what would be involved in pursuing this. I said that Maddy's mental health was not strong at present but that I would see what happened over the next week, when hopefully she would be feeling better, and be back in touch.

During that week, Maddy received another phone call from the young man who had previously received the filthy messages from someone claiming to be Maddy. He asked whether she had contacted him again. Maddy replied that if she wanted to call him she would do it from her own phone, not from a silent number. He acknowledged that the girl from the group must be up to her tricks again.

The following weekend Maddy hosted a birthday celebration for one of her friends at our home. Maddy's friend received a menacing call from one of the bullies asking why she had not been invited. At this stage, these girls were now young adults.

I spoke to Maddy's friend about this incident and Maddy's friend confirmed what Maddy had told me. Maddy's friend told me that after this night she deleted and blocked them from all social media. This lovely young lady woke up the next morning to hate texts saying she was ruining her life for Maddy and losing all her friends, so why would she choose to stick by Maddy?

I recall Maddy calling me in tears saying that someone had put her name and phone number on an advertisement selling festival tickets that she knew nothing about. There were lots of calls, people were cross with her and abusing her because she did not have the tickets. Maddy was in a panic. Again, I called the police. As they had already been piecing together a case of harassment, they advised that they could track the computer IP number so that they could pay the house a visit to discuss the fraud.

Maddy was in extreme distress at this stage and I was still contemplating whether, or not, I wanted to go as far as putting restraining orders on these young women, when three of the members of the group turned up on our property. They were looking for clothes and alcohol that had been left at our house months before. Two of them stayed in the car, while one came into our home, uninvited, demanding that I give her the alcohol and clothes. I said we did not have anything of theirs, and she asked to look through Maddy's room. By this stage I was angry at her lack of respect and invasion of our privacy. I told her to leave our house.

During the interaction, my husband and I went to their car which was parked outside our house. We took the opportunity to confront them about their knowledge, if any, of the egging of our house. One of the young women was so shocked by the confrontation that she owned up to my husband that she had egged another girl's house previously.

I mentioned, quite firmly, that I knew about all the harassment they had been inflicting on Maddy. I advised them that the police knew about the harassing text message, the fact that our house got egged the next day, the fact that one of the women had been talking filth to the young man who texted Maddy, and that the police were also investigating who was responsible for the fraudulent advertisement. I advised them that we gave the police a list of names of whom we suspected were involved, based on Maddy's previous bullying experiences, social media and mobile evidence. I said that if they did not stop harassing us that I would get restraining orders put on all of them.

The young woman who had confessed to egging another girl's house was particularly upset. Over the years she was the one that had caused the most pain to Maddy, or at least, hers was the name I heard most often. I could never understand how this young woman could make Maddy believe she was so worthless. Maddy was everything this young woman was not.

The other two occupants of the car seemed completely ambivalent, one of them was smirking as they drove off.

Personally, it felt good to finally confront them. It felt good that their names had been recorded with the police, that the police knew of the previous incidents and what Maddy had suffered over the years. It felt good to know that the police were collecting evidence, knowing that the bullies were now aware that there were consequences for those actions – it was the most satisfying feeling.

Maddy did not feel this way. Maddy left the house devastated that we had confronted the bullies and brought it all out in the open. I remember her running down the street barefoot and hysterical. Maddy feared that we had made things worse for her. I finally got hold of Maddy. She had gone to meet a girlfriend who she was very close to. Maddy had talked to her, and this girlfriend had calmed her down. I tried to explain to Maddy that this was a good thing, that they finally were confronted and knew that there would be consequences for their actions if they did not stop bullying her. Maddy felt guilty that her father and I had to get involved, guilty that our house had been egged, she felt that it was all her fault. Maddy often felt guilty, even when she had nothing to feel guilty about, this was part of her anxiety.

Later that evening I was contacted by the mother of one of the young women. The mother was angry that her daughter had been accused of egging our house. I explained that we had not accused her daughter, that we had asked her about her knowledge of it, and that it was her daughter who had confessed to egging someone else's house. The mother said, "what sort of people are you that attack children in the street?" I replied that they were no longer children. I explained that all the events coincided with her daughter's nasty text message to Maddy. I explained that I was over it all, and that I wanted them to leave Maddy alone. I remember, clearly, the mother of this young woman stating that her daughter did not have "a bad bone in her body" and that I was mistaken. She was confused as to why I went to the police and not to her. I felt in complete bewilderment that this woman was so blind to her daughter's behaviour. It also left me cold as I realised that none of the young women, nor their parents, were ever spoken to by the school regarding the bullying incidents that I had reported, as this mother was oblivious to what her daughter had been inflicting on others for so many years.

I formed the opinion that the mother of this young woman looked at her daughter through rose-coloured glasses, so nothing I could say would change that. At the time, I felt that it would be pointless going to her, that her daughter had been left unchecked for too many years for her parents to make a difference at this late stage. These young women were now adults who faced adult consequences.

After these bullying incidents, I noticed wounds on Maddy's arms, not from any attempt to end her life but more from a self-harm perspective. Thinking back, I had seen similar wounds before, at different times over the years as she was growing up, but Maddy had always made an excuse for the wounds that I believed. I asked her about the wounds, but she would not talk to me about them. I pleaded with her to get professional help. Maddy refused.

I cannot deny that, at times, I have wished for all the bad karma that the universe could inflict, to rain down on the young women that bullied Maddy. Unfortunately, those feelings would not help me or Maddy. The biggest favour I could do for myself was to forgive them and hope that the nightmare was behind us. Maddy struggled with this, she could not understand how I could ever expect her to forgive them, but it was the only way that I could see the cycle of pain to be broken.

After Maddy died, I was told by more than one person that these girls had been bullying children since primary school. Maddy started at her secondary school in 2008. Bullying did not have such a high profile as it does now. We were at a loss as a family about how to deal with the bullying issue. However, I do believe that if the school had worked with the children when they were younger, things may have been different for all of them as adults. If the school had spoken to the parents about the incidents, if the school had supported and protected Maddy, if the parents, children and school had worked together to assist the children to feel empathy, and have healthy relationships with each other, perhaps the adult bullying would never have occurred.

*"Without intervention, a significant number of youth who bully in childhood will continue to bully as they move through adolescence and into adulthood. As children mature, the nature of bullying changes. From early adolescence, new forms of aggression emerge. With developing thinking and social skills, children become aware of others' vulnerabilities and of their own power relative to others."*

Source: PREVNet

# Chapter 5

## MADDY'S FINAL CHAPTER

**OUR CONFRONTATION SEEMED** to work, life was quiet, for a time.

Maddy started university and did very well. I always said that a pass was good enough but she would not be happy without, at the very least, a credit. Maddy was a high achiever, she honestly believed this would make people like her more.

Maddy had a couple of failed relationships over the following years. Maddy continued to struggle with anxiety, and whenever anything went wrong she would just go back to that place of self-loathing and negative self-talk.

A shining light in Maddy's life was the job she secured at a private college teaching in their early learning centre. The age group Maddy taught was three and four year old children. Maddy was so proud of her job. I often said that teaching children was the best career for her, children are accepting, they do not judge and could not hurt her.

As Maddy was studying a disability component as part of her degree, the centre allocated a young boy who had autism to her care. Maddy bonded quickly with this little boy. They became close and he responded well to Maddy's attention. Maddy would often come home and tell me

about his progress and she kept a book for herself to remind her of his achievements.

Maddy received good feedback from the senior teaching staff about her relationship with the little boy, and the improvement in his development. When the little boy had to leave the centre at the end of the year, Maddy was so upset, crying and miserable. Maddy said to me "Mum I don't think I can do this job if I have to say goodbye to the children, it makes me too sad". I assured her it would get easier with time. It didn't really, she always got attached.

After studying two years of her degree, Maddy's anxiety got the better of her and she did not want to go on with her study. Maddy said that she did not like who she became when she studied, as the pressure was too much for her. I was exhausted myself after two years of the stress and anxiety on all of us because of the study, so I agreed that it was the right decision for her to defer.

Maddy continued with her job and was eventually made a permanent staff member, she was very proud. Maddy would do the most amazing things when she had to plan sessions for the children. Maddy would sit with her computer for hours, looking at different things that she thought the children would enjoy, that fitted with the curriculum or subject matter that they were learning about.

Maddy's perfectionist nature increased each year. Sometimes just organising what she was going to wear took forever. Maddy strived for perfectionism in everything she did. Close enough was never good enough and that is how she treated everything in her life.

I remember when Maddy had her first performance review. In Maddy's performance development review she said that she had received feedback for an area that needed her attention. The feedback was regarding a personality conflict and the person had made a complaint against Maddy. Maddy told me later that she felt like she was being bullied all over again.

Maddy believed that the complaint was not justified, and her side of things were not considered. Maddy said she was so offended when her supervisor raised the issue, that she left crying and upset all the children. I said to Maddy that performance reviews were part of working, that it was not personal, and that there would have been many positive things said to her by her supervisor. Maddy could not remember, she said all that she heard were the negative comments.

None of us truly knows what battles the people in our lives are struggling with, so treating every individual with tolerance and empathy is important.

When Maddy was upset and had her anxiety attacks, she would get so angry at herself for the situation she found herself in. I sometimes despair myself at what horrible things she must have said to herself in those challenging times. This was part of her anxiety and her perfectionist nature, most problems that were trivial to most were monumental to her.

*When Maddy was upset and had her anxiety attacks, she would get so angry at herself for the situation she found herself in.*

We did get through these events in Maddy's life by having many conversations until she got to a place of acceptance. We had lots of hugs and I tried to give her reassurance and positivity. I did everything I could to try to let her lead a happy life.

In 2015, Maddy told me she had met some young men, and their partners, who played in one of the state league football teams. One night they came over for a gathering at our house. I noticed one of the boys looking at Maddy. This young man was looking at her constantly. I asked Maddy about him but she dismissed any affection toward him, saying they were just friends. In time Maddy noticed the way he looked at her too, and they began their relationship.

They became inseparable. Maddy's anxiety was always just under the surface, and they were not without difficulties in their relationship. However, I could see that he loved her and she loved him.

Maddy became very close with her partner's family. Maddy's partner has an Italian heritage with a big family. Maddy always wanted to be part of a big family and was very close to his parents, brothers and grandparents, as well as the wider family unit. Maddy thought the world of her partner's family and loved being part of it. Maddy got her wish for a big family.

Maddy loved food, I was not the only one that wondered how she kept her slim figure with all the food that she ate. Going out with someone with Italian heritage and getting to eat the gourmet food, it was a match made in Heaven for Maddy.

You may think, at least Maddy did not have any further encounter with the bullies that were the catalyst for her anxiety and issues in life. Unfortunately, the story does not have a happy ending for our Maddy.

Maddy told me that she had run into one of the young women from the group of bullies who admitted to her that they were horrible to her. They were in their early twenties at this stage. This young woman was the one that smirked when Maddy's father and I confronted her, when the bullying was at its worst. This young woman dismissed her behaviour, and that of others, as "just what kids do". There was more to it than that for Maddy. Those incidents of bullying had left Maddy with psychological trauma. Maddy could not understand how this young woman could dismiss how much pain the group caused her through school and afterwards. Maddy said to me at the time that she wanted to write each of them a letter to tell them how much they hurt her, the damage that they caused her psychologically and physically, effecting all aspects of her life.

Maddy and her partner went overseas early in 2017. Maddy desperately wanted to see other places, and I am pleased she got to do this. I never really worried about her safety during this holiday as I knew Maddy's partner would take care of her.

Maddy had the time of her life and came back more in love and happy than I had ever seen her.

Later that year Maddy had a fun night with her partner and his mates at a dress up party. Later that night they went into town with friends to help celebrate a birthday. A father of one of the young men associated with the group of bullies was at the entrance to the nightclub. He said to Maddy, "you don't really want to go down there, do you?". Maddy just thought he was drunk and did not pay any attention to him.

When Maddy walked into the room, most of the group of bullies, her ex-boyfriend and some of their parents were in the club. Without provocation, and bear in mind all Maddy had done was walk into the room - one of the bullies that had tormented her all through school and afterwards, walked up to her and threw a drink in her face. Maddy retaliated by throwing her drink at the woman. Maddy advised that one of these women had said to her "why don't you just kill yourself?"

One of the young men in Maddy's group had a go at one of the young men in the bully's group, Maddy's partner tried to talk to some of the other women in the bully's group – it all spiralled out of control. The damage had already been done. Maddy was heartbroken.

The people that bullied Maddy were at the club for a birthday celebration for one of the people in their group. I am still astonished that there were parents in the room who knew Maddy's history with this group and nobody helped her. The father at the entrance, knew enough to make the comment, yet he did not try to stop her from going downstairs to the club. He could have warned her that they were all downstairs. What sort of society creates people like this? These are questions I am left with.

The next day, after the attack in the night club, Maddy and her partner told me about what had happened. Maddy's partner told me that he had underestimated how much these people had made Maddy suffer - he said he had "never witnessed any people be so vicious to another person who had not provoked it."

On one level Maddy was glad that her partner had witnessed it. Maddy told me that at least he knows now that I am not being a "drama queen." Maddy said that she was so embarrassed that it happened in front of some of their parents. I said to Maddy that it was the parents who should feel shame for not intervening. I told Maddy that she had to move forward, that to live a good life, then she would win and the bullies would lose. I will remember her reply for the rest of my days. Maddy said, "it is too late Mum, they have ruined me". Maddy never recovered psychologically from this event.

After this attack, I noticed self-harm wounds on Maddy's arm and discovered a knife with blood on it in her room. I pleaded with Maddy to get professional help, Maddy refused to talk about the self-harm any further. I remember being frightened at the sight of the wounds, and called Lifeline. They said that self-harm was to release the emotional pain and it did not mean that she wanted to end her life. I also called her doctor to ask that she speak with Maddy next time she came in as I was not able to get through to her.

With love and support and lots of chatting about this event, Maddy did seem to move on from it. Maddy did not speak of it as much. At least that is how it appeared. Maddy became skilled at appearances and hiding the truth of how she felt.

Maddy once told me that she felt fake. That her smiles and efforts to be happy were not truly her. Maddy said that her reality was a dark and lonely place at times. To everyone else Maddy appeared to have it all and was in control of her life. It was only those closest to her that truly knew her struggles and the trauma that bullying caused her.

Maddy and I had many discussions in the last two years of her life about whether, or not, she should go back to finish her degree. Maddy really did not want the stress of studying again but felt that she would not progress in her career if she did not finish her studies. I did not want her to go back to study as I remembered how bad her anxiety was in those two years of university study after high school.

Maddy was worried about her career progression. In 2018 Maddy went back to study part time. Maddy picked up a couple of subjects and I thought this workload would be manageable for her. Maddy had moments where she was stressed about it but she seemed to be coping OK. I remember not long before she died she texted me to say she had got two distinctions and a high distinction – she was so very happy. I was very proud of her but a pass would have made me equally as proud.

In the first half of 2018 my husband got sick with salmonella poisoning. This incapacitated him for three months. During this time, I had to manage our home by myself. Maddy was off living her life and spent much of her time with her partner. My son was busy with his sporting commitments and doing his year twelve. I was working nearly full time and knew that I had a big project at work to take on midway through the year. My husband and I decided to move to a smaller, more manageable property.

Maddy had lived most of her life in our big home, we had lots of parties and family events there. Maddy loved this home. Change of any kind was something she struggled with and her anxiety caused grief during this process for her and our family.

We purchased our new home by the beach, and our other house sold quickly. I did not burden Maddy with any of the stress of the actual move, allowing her to get her head around everything. Maddy finally got to see the house that we had bought and she loved it. Maddy started talking to me about how she wanted to decorate her new room, what curtains I was thinking of, I sought her thoughts on everything and tried to include her as much as I could. When we finally moved into our new home, Maddy was happy and relaxed.

One afternoon Maddy sat with my husband and me in our new front courtyard enjoying the sun and nibbling on a cheese platter that I had prepared. It was a beautiful afternoon and we chatted about all sorts of things. Maddy talked about some of the issues she was having at the time, we discussed strategies and she said that she was coping OK.

I had noticed during the couple of months preceding her death that Maddy's behaviour on some fronts had changed slightly. Maddy seemed to fly off into an anxiety attack over the most trivial things. What appeared to be small insignificant incidents would often push her to her limit.

The stressful exertion of emotions would often leave Maddy physically exhausted at the end of the day. Maddy always complained of feeling tired. I believe Maddy was not aware of the impact her mental health had on her physical health.

I just put it down to the fact that we were moving, Maddy had assignments due, and that she was trying to cope with change. Maddy also withdrew from me, and the family during that time. I was not getting as many text messages.

Maddy was punishing herself at the gym and would often complain to me about her figure and that she felt fat – she was tiny. I remember the week before she died, Maddy had a melt down over some x-rays that I could not find. Maddy said I was a terrible mother because I could not find them, and later apologised. This was how our relationship had always been, in many ways I was the person she took everything out on. Maddy knew that no matter how she treated me, I would always forgive her, always love her.

I now know that it was not Maddy but her mental health illness that caused her to say the terrible things that she said to me over the years. Sometimes I felt like Maddy was two different people.

Maddy's kindness and generosity was always most prevalent when it was time to give gifts. Maddy loved celebrating Christmas and birthdays, and even though buying presents caused her stress, as she always worried that people would not like what she bought, she always spent a fortune. Maddy was very generous. Maddy was an extremely good saver, she would say that this was one area of her life that she had control over, and she loved to see her bank balance grow. Prior to Maddy's death she was talking about investing her money into shares or property.

According to Beyond Blue people "use drugs and alcohol as a coping strategy." One of the most frequent conversations I had with Maddy before she went out socialising was over drinking alcohol. Maddy rarely had a drink during the week but would binge drink when she went out. I always suspected this relaxed her and gave her courage to socialise, she liked to fit in with what everyone else was doing. Maddy had commented to me on several occasions that she always had a fear of running into the bullies when she was out. I would say to her that drinking alcohol was the worst thing she could do for her anxiety. After a party or night out, it often took her a couple of days to get back to a good place with her anxiety, but Maddy rarely listened to me on this subject.

The night before Maddy died we sat on the lounge and laughed and talked about her day. Maddy rolled around with the Pugs and was in a very upbeat mood. Maddy said that she really did not want to go out that night. I suggested that she stay home and watch a movie with the Pugs, and

we would not be out for dinner for long. I often worried about Maddy's safety when she socialised with the group of young women she was going out with. Maddy had not known them for a great length of time, and I had heard things from her that concerned me. On one occasion Maddy came home distressed as she had gone out with them, and they had left her in the bathroom of a night club while they all caught a cab to another location without telling her, leaving her alone. I asked her not to go out. Maddy said "if I don't go out with them, they will not invite me anymore." I said that she was behaving just like she was at school, that fear of missing out drove her rather than choosing where and with whom she would be safest spending her time with. I had to drop my son to work and by the time I got home, Maddy was gone, I never saw her again.

In the early morning that Maddy took her own life, she was alone. For reasons that are still unknown to me, Maddy decided to stay at the house of a woman who was more of an acquaintance than a friend, instead of meeting up with her partner. Maddy and the other woman were both under the influence of alcohol and there was an argument. I have heard various versions of what happened that night, but whatever the course of events I have chosen not to investigate, I do not want to know, it would never bring her back.

Once Maddy's anxiety took hold it was quite often difficult to reason with her. Maddy would get angry, angry at herself, angry at the situation, and she would become difficult to communicate with at these times. If you added alcohol to the mix, it was nearly impossible to get through to her. Maddy's panic attacks inevitably surfaced, and her spiral in behaviour resulted.

Maddy obviously wanted to get out of the situation she found herself in with the woman she had been socialising with. Maddy got into her car to drive home. Knowing that Maddy would have been over the alcohol limit, the woman called the police. This young woman did not know about

Maddy's anxiety, but with the two of them being under the influence of alcohol, I am guessing neither of them could process their choices logically.

The police arrested Maddy for drink driving and released her an hour later, in her pyjamas, alone and still over the legal limit for alcohol. I do believe the police should never have let her leave their premises alone. To my knowledge, Maddy had never even had a speeding fine before. Maddy spent her life trying to be perfect. This would have been an enormous set-back for her emotionally and psychologically. With Maddy's anxiety she would have been in a terribly distressed state.

When I spoke to the police I asked why they could not detain her until someone was able to pick her up. The police advised me that they could not detain her as she was an adult and she wanted to leave. As she had not been driving dangerously and had not presented as obviously intoxicated, they did not think there was a problem letting her go.

The police do campaigning to watch out for drunk walkers, and yet they let a young woman who had just blown over the legal limit for alcohol walk onto the street in the early hours of the morning, without any support. The State Coroner decided to investigate the circumstances around Maddy's death. The State Coroner found that the police had no culpability that night. They may have followed due process, but I still believe from a viewpoint of human empathy they missed the mark.

It has since become obvious that in the months leading up to Maddy's death, her mental health issues were a challenge for her. Many things went wrong for Maddy on that last day. There were obvious stresses in her life at that time. With the pressure of the events of that morning, being under the influence of alcohol, being alone, fearful, and no doubt the resultant self-loathing, anxiety and negative self-talk that were part of Maddy's dialogue on most days, Maddy would have felt broken. Maddy made the decision to take her own life.

Before we received the devastating news, it had already been a long day. Maddy's partner and I were in constant contact. I had had a very short conversation with Maddy in the morning that led to a disagreement. Maddy told me that something terrible had happened and she had lost her licence for 12 months. I was so frustrated with her, I scolded her. Maddy did not give me any details, I did not know she was alone. I could not get through to her, she was not listening to anything I was saying, she called me a terrible mother. As it was not uncommon for her to say this, I did not give it a second thought, but as the day progressed without any word from her to anyone, I started to feel sick and fear that something terrible had happened to her. As it turned out, those were the last words she ever spoke to me.

# Chapter 6

# THE DEVASTATION

**WHEN I ARRIVED** home on the day that Maddy died, Lochie said he could see a man in a suit in our lounge room. I could see from our back yard, there were two of our good friends in the family room. Our good friends were always there for us in a crisis, I loved them, but my heart sank. Words cannot express the pain of losing your child. Sometimes I can still hear my screams at that dreadful moment I was told she had gone. You know a part of you has gone forever and you wonder what your life will resemble without that child in it.

You hear people say, no parent should ever have to outlive their child. Until it happened to me I never, really understood the magnitude of this statement. It is the cruellest experience, the pain is so severe, I could not imagine how I would ever recover.

I had such a tsunami of feelings. As Maddy took her own life, I was left wondering why? Why had she done this? How could she do this to me? How could she do this to her father and brother, my mother who she adored? How could she do this to her partner and his family? I had no answers. I had so much guilt about my last conversation with her. If I had shown her more understanding, if I had comforted her instead of being frustrated with her, would any of this have mattered? Would she not have made that final decision?

I realised as time went on that it really was not about us. Maddy did not do it to hurt us. Maddy was angry at herself, at the circumstances, the pain she felt in her mind, her negative self-talk, she wanted to end the suffering for herself at that moment, she did not think about how it would affect everyone else. Maddy's anxiety left her with no resources to process the predicament she found herself in.

Over the years Maddy suffered from anxiety, she would say that we would all be better off if she were not here. Every time something bad happened in Maddy's life, Maddy would go back to that place of despair, that dark place she lived in for so many years when she was being bullied. My stomach still churns when I think of the terrible things that she would have been saying to herself in the last moments of her life.

In the weeks after Maddy died we received hundreds of condolence notes, cards, flowers, food and visitors. I felt more and more pain at the realisation, that Maddy had caused all this heartache for other people. The amount of people this had affected left me numb. There was the ripple effect to her death – my husband, my son, her partner, my mother, our extended family, our friends, their children, her partner's friends and family, her friends, the staff from the school she taught at, the children she taught, the parents of the children she taught - the list just seemed to go on and on. That ripple effect vibrated through my life like a clashing cymbal that I never thought I would be free of.

I felt more and more pain at the realisation, that Maddy had caused all this heartache for other people.

We had so much support. I was humbled and overwhelmed at times to think of how kind people were to us. There were so many things we struggled with at that time. It was a blur. We had the police harassing us for statements and we had to identify Maddy's body after her death. One of our good friends offered to identify her body so that we did not have to suffer that pain. He had known Maddy since she was born and I know how hard that was for him. There are just some things you do not ever think you will have to do as a friend. To this day we are so grateful for the support we received from those that love us.

I did not know where to begin to organise, or even think about a funeral for my child. This was another issue that I had to battle with in my exhaustion. I did not want to have a funeral, rather have a priest bless her and then put her to rest privately. With the outpouring of grief from all parts of our lives and how her death affected so many other people, we decided to give her a funeral and open it up to whomever wanted to attend. This was a struggle in so many ways, I couldn't sleep and I barely ate. I felt constantly sick.

The following words may not resonate with some people who choose to read this book, but this is what I believe, and this is what gave me comfort.

Strange things happened in those following weeks, some may say they were coincidence, some may say I was just looking for things that were not there, but I believe to this day that our loved ones are around us.

My sister was not going to tell me about a dream that she had as she did not want to hurt me further. I wanted to know, there was not really anything else that could hurt me at this point.

My sister had offered to close Maddy's casket on the day of the funeral as I didn't want that memory. I wanted to hold happy memories of the last time I saw her beautiful face, on the night before she died, playing with the Pugs. My sister adored Maddy, for her to have to do this was so difficult and I struggled with the thought of the pain that this would cause her, and my brother-in-law, but I was so grateful.

My sister told me that in the dream that she had, it was time to identify Maddy in the casket. My sister went up to Maddy and kissed her on the forehead and she said in the dream that Maddy woke up. On the day of the funeral my sister went up to Maddy and kissed her on the forehead, as she had done in the dream.

I could feel tears well in my eyes. I said to my sister already knowing the answer, "did you know that is where I kissed her every night before we went to sleep?" My sister, of course, had no idea. This was something between Maddy and me, not even my husband knew. I remember a letter Maddy sent to me once where she told me that when I kissed her on the forehead, I made everything all better.

With the plans for the funeral, I desperately wanted it to be in our local church and the service done by the priest. The priest ironically had been the priest at Maddy's primary school and knew her. I am sure this was also a difficult event for him, but he was wonderful. One of those angels that helped us through that dark period in our lives.

The only time he had that week was on the Wednesday, 4th July 2018 or we would have to wait another week for the funeral. We chose that day.

That day had significance, that was the tenth anniversary of my father's death. Was that coincidence? I like to think that was a sign that she was with my Dad.

A lady I knew from childhood, in fact probably one of the oldest friends I have, bobbed back into my world when Maddy died. This lady is a police woman and our friendship is one that is always there even though it may be months in between our communication. We had times in our lives that ran parallel, particularly when both of our children were suffering from bullying and subsequent mental health issues.

The support she gave me personally is beyond measure. From the day Maddy died she sent me a quote every day. It was the one thing I could count on, it made a difference as trivial as it sounds.

My sister and I talk on the phone regularly, my mother and I talk every day. I walk with a friend and our dogs every morning. My friend listens to my every thought with love and no judgement. I have another friend I car pool with. Our car rides are spent chatting and processing all parts of our lives. I have a Monday lunch friend and a Tuesday lunch friend. We also chat about life and all of this helps us to belong and feel valued and connected to each other.

I remember having lunch with my Tuesday lunch friend one day. We were chatting about Maddy's bullying experiences and her death. We had spent an hour talking about all sorts of things. A lady came up to me and held my arm. The lady had overheard our conversation. The lady said that her husband had taken his life two years previously. The lady said that she did not have anyone to talk to at that time, and how lucky I was to have such a good friend to talk to. I felt so sad for her, it made me realise that I was not the only one who was suffering, and that there were people far worse off than me. Talking to the people I love truly has been my saviour.

I have a work family. At the time Maddy died, I had a work associate in the office next to me. He listened to me, and supported me when I had those inevitable days where I struggled. He would check on me several times a day. We had many conversations and he always seemed to have insight into how I was feeling and what to say to help me. I had wonderful staff that knew just the time when I needed a hug.

As horrific as that time was, things slipped into place, we got the support we needed and the love of family, friends, people we hardly knew, and the wider community, carried us along. Even my local coffee lady would drop by with food and coffee for us. There really are so many kind and caring people in this world.

During those nights leading up to the funeral, I would wake up in the night, feeling alone in the dark with a sick feeling in the pit of my stomach that Maddy had gone, I would always wake up crying. I just wanted that feeling to end.

One night just before waking I had a dream. I was in a cave, it was so dark and I was so scared. There were black rocks surrounding me. Through the darkness, I could see a light in the distance. As I approached closer to the light I saw a beautiful flower growing out of the dark rocks. It was pure white, with a golden glow around it, almost like a halo. I was so happy that I found this flower, that it ended my darkness and that it lit my way. From that day forward the sick feeling ended. Every time I woke up I remembered, and focused on the happiness I felt when I saw the flower in my dream. I like to think the flower was a gift from Maddy.

These are the experiences that helped me, that gave me hope that she was happy and not suffering, that she was now safe and loved without any pain. Nobody could hurt her anymore. These thoughts continue to give me comfort. As much as I miss Maddy, I no longer have the worry, I know she is at peace and this gives me peace.

*Chapter 7*

# THE FUNERAL

**I KNEW MADDY,** and had doubts about whether a funeral in a church would have been what she wanted. I knew she believed in God, she had told me once. Maddy was young, and a church funeral with organ music and hymns did not seem the right fit for Maddy.

I was determined that her funeral was going to be amazing, as she was amazing. It became very clear to me over those weeks, just what an impact her life had on others so the funeral needed to be something special.

I had put the word out that I would talk of Maddy's bullying in the eulogy I wrote. I did not think for a minute that the bullies would show their faces at Maddy's funeral. They were horrible to her in life, why would they want to respect her in death? I was not in the frame of mind to see any of them, and I wanted to ensure the funeral was full of love and peace.

I did not know what music to choose, Maddy's taste in music at times was quite unique. I sat down one day and just scrolled through music on the internet. I knew I wanted a lullaby that I sung to her as a baby "You are my sunshine". I found a rendition of it by a young woman called Jasmine Thompson. This song had such significance as I would sing it to her every night and did so while she grew. Maddy was the most superb baby and that song still brings back happy memories for me. I also wanted

"Somewhere over the Rainbow" and found a rendition which was modern and was sung by Eva Cassidy. From there all the songs just popped up in my search, again it all fell into place.

I suspected from the outpouring of grief that there would be a couple of hundred people at the funeral so we had 300 memorial cards and church service pamphlets printed just to make sure. As it turned out that was nowhere near enough.

On the day of the funeral I was numb, it was almost like I had cried a river of tears and I had no more to give. I dreaded having to see all those people, to suffer through the grief with them, to see their pain, pain that my daughter had caused. I felt such a mountain of emotions that I just wanted to curl up in a corner and never deal with any of it again.

My husband had not coped at all since she died, so I was not able to share my feelings with him. I felt like I had to be strong for him and my son. My son never left my side, even though he was in pain himself, he comforted me and gave me the strength I needed to face that terrible day.

Our home was around the corner from our church, but it was the longest walk of my life. I could see people starting to queue to go into the church.

We had to face it, we walked down the long corridor from the back of the church. The pews were starting to fill. Maddy's white casket lay in the centre of the altar, beautiful pink roses covering her casket, her partner's football scarf laying at the foot of the casket.

Many people came up to hug us and pass their sympathy to us, it was a wave of emotions that I struggled with. Maddy's service was beautiful, we honoured her as she deserved. There were many people who asked why. I went through her journey in life, the bullying, her battles with anxiety, self-esteem and being a perfectionist. I believe that the eulogy helped people to understand the detrimental, lasting trauma that bullying had on Maddy and her psychological health.

Maddy's partner spoke his own words about her and their life together. Maddy's gorgeous girlfriends got up to speak, and talk about their fun times with her. What a good friend she was, how funny and smart she was and how she loved food. In fact, there were so many stories about Maddy and food, it still makes me smile.

At the end of the service, the funeral director asked the audience to stand and give Maddy a final round of applause to show their respect. The applause thundered through the church, it was so loud.

I felt ill when it came to putting the petals on Maddy's casket, and having to say my final goodbye. I felt weak and distraught. I remember resting my head on her casket crying, thinking that it was not going to be possible for me to part from her. One of my beautiful friends walked over to me, put her arms around me and helped me out of the church. Her help allowed me to settle down ready to greet the hundreds of people that queued to pass their condolences to us.

I was astonished, and overwhelmed at the amount of people who came to her funeral. I really did not know the huge social connections Maddy had made in her life. I was told that there were over 500 people at the service. It was standing room only, they overflowed out into the foyer of the church. Pride replaced the pain I felt. I finally realised what an impact her life had on others. It was confirmed to me on so many levels that I had raised a wonderful person, that her gifts were many and her life would have a lasting impact on those that had the privilege of knowing her, and loving her.

How sad that Maddy felt alone a lot of the time in life, that she continually feared that people did not like her, that she was not worthy of love.

Maddy had a high drive to be perfect. Maddy's perfectionist nature came from wanting people to like her. If I am perfect, if my life is perfect, if I look perfect then maybe people will like me. This was her self-talk. The trouble with being a perfectionist is it gives you a long way to fall.

Some say that we each go to our own funeral, I hope so, I hope she was pleased. My son ironically had a dream that Maddy was sitting alongside of us at the funeral with my father. I hope she was there, I hope she knows now, how very much she was loved.

*Chapter 8*

# HEALING

**WHEN A LOVED** one dies and you suffer such extreme loss, it is hard to imagine that there is any possibility of healing. Will life ever be the same again? Will I ever be happy again?

For me the answer is yes and no. No, life will never be the same again but yes you can be happy again.

Once the numbness has passed, and you get through those most difficult stages, life goes on. The normal life you knew has gone forever. A new normal has taken over. It can be a good normal, a happy normal. It is just a different normal.

People would say to me, "you are coping so well, I don't know how you can do that". Then I would feel guilty that perhaps I was not grieving properly for her. Should I have been different? Should I have rolled up in a corner and not functioned for 6 months or 12 months?

I came to understand that there is no right or wrong way to grieve. Each of us go through a mountain of different emotions depending on our own relationship with the person who has passed.

My son's grief was different to my husband's grief, my grief was different to both of theirs.

For me, I know I did everything I could for her. I know I could not have done anything more. Every decision I made, I thought was the right one for Maddy at the time. I know I loved her more than my own life and would have given mine to save hers. That is the love of a mother.

I did suffer regret and guilt over our last conversation that took me many months to reconcile. At the end of the day, I could only act on the information Maddy gave me. I did not know Maddy was alone, I thought she was with her partner as she always was. I did not know she was still under the influence of alcohol, she did not sound that way, I did not know any of the circumstances around what had put her in that final place of desperation.

> *I wanted to feel it all. Every sick feeling, every desperate emotion, every tear – I had to feel all of that to get through it.*

As a parent, we can only raise our children to the best of our ability, when they become adults their choices, and the consequences of those choices become their own. Maddy's mental health issues, in many cases, were prohibitive of her making sensible decisions at times. However, Maddy could have made many alternative decisions over the years that were more sensible for her mental health. Maddy could have sought professional help. Maddy could have made different choices in friends, partners and lifestyle choices. Maddy could have made different choices on that final night. Unfortunately, Maddy always felt that she did not deserve happiness and ultimately this often led to poor decision-making capacity. At the end of the day, the decisions she made, no matter what the reasons, were her own and I just had to accept that fact.

I rarely consumed much alcohol, but at the time Maddy died I decided that I would not drink alcohol while I was healing. This turned out to be a blessing. It allowed me to feel everything. There was no substance I took to take away the pain. I wanted to feel it all. Every sick feeling, every desperate emotion, every tear – I had to feel all of that to get through it.

After the funeral, I slept like a baby. Sleep was the best thing as it had been broken for so long. My appetite returned and I started to feel well again. We live close to the beach and I found walking along the beach grounded me, and being close to nature gave me peace.

In addition to staying away from artificial substances, getting enough sleep, eating well and talking to those I loved, I wrote a journal. It just seemed to help. At the time, my mind was in complete turmoil and I thought I would explode, it helped me to write things down, and to put my thoughts in order. I would write quotes, important lines from books that I wanted to remember and positive things that I heard. I read somewhere that there was scientific evidence that showed how gratitude increased happiness and decreased depressive symptoms.

Gratitude became a daily practice for me. I believe it has helped me with resilience and positivity moving forward. Putting pen to paper helped me to put my emotions in order, it alleviated my stress and helped me to have a positive mindset every day. Although I do not find the need to journal much now, I have gone back to it periodically to read the pages of my journal to see how far I have come. I do continue with one practice I learned during that terrible time, and that is to be grateful every day for the blessings that I have, and I have many.

My husband found going back to work and trying to pick up his routines worked for him. For my son, it was similar, get back to the routines of life. My son was doing year twelve, he had his sport and his friends who rallied around him. My nephews were never far away and were a great support for him. I preferred to be alone with my animals, read, watch television, have coffee with people that wanted to drop by. There were so many visitors during that period that I was never truly alone.

I read many books during this time. I read self-help books, near death experience books; in many ways these gave me comfort, if only to hear other people's stories. Sometimes when you hear the stories of others, your story does not seem so bad.

Suffering in life does not discriminate and we all face it at some point, it is part of life. It is the kindness and empathy of others that will get you through. Never lose hope, there is always hope. Even if it is the hope that you will feel better, isn't that something to look forward to?

It is OK to feel happiness. In fact, when you first experience happiness after tragedy, it is so intense because it has been a foreign emotion for so long. I remember my son won the grand final with his soccer team. I was team manager, I also got a medal. My goodness, the happiness this day gave us is indescribable. We had family and friends cheering him and his team mates on, it was an amazing experience. You may think, it is such a trivial thing in the whole scheme of the events at that time, but when you have had such sadness, to feel joy again is better than anything you can imagine. I felt no guilt about being happy. In fact, I felt in my heart of hearts that this was what Maddy would have wanted for us – to be happy again. When you love people, you only ever want them to be happy.

I found talking the best medicine for me. I talked to anyone who wanted to listen. I decided to talk to the people that made me feel uplifted in some way. I surrounded myself with positive people who loved me.

When I find myself going through the what if questions or back into the past where the pain lives, I stop it in my mind. I speak to myself with positivity and remind myself that it was all beyond my control. If you say words in your mind often enough, eventually they become your truth. I go to my happy place and bring myself back to the present in my mind. The mind is a powerful thing. I found meditation worked for me. Before my father died he taught me a white light meditation and I still use that often when I need to find peace.

Maddy often referred to her work colleagues as her work family. Maddy was so happy in her job with the children. It was obvious to me that these people truly loved her. I remain in contact with her closest work friend, and I am very grateful for that. Her friend told Maddy the Friday before she died that she was pregnant. Maddy came home so excited, of course she already knew and was like a cat on a hot tin roof waiting for her friend to tell her. I am glad that she found out before she died.

The principal of the school where Maddy worked had been a wonderful support. His text messages were comforting. He even offered their church for Maddy's service.

Maddy's primary school principal came to her funeral. I thought this was just lovely. Maddy loved her primary school and the teaching staff. He sat and mourned for her with the hundreds of other people. Maddy's primary school years were her happiest school years.

I was advised by many past students who attended the funeral, that there was no representation by Maddy's secondary school. This added to my grief at the time. I felt that Maddy did not matter in life to them, and in her death, she also did not matter to them. We did have a representative contact us on behalf of the Principal at the time of Maddy's death, and received the obligatory, "sorry for your loss" and they offered pastoral care to my son when he returned to school.

To this day I have never had any communication from the Principal of Maddy's school, and he never met with my son, even though my son was doing his year twelve the year Maddy died. Between my two children, we spent 10 years at that school, and he could not take the time to ring me or meet with my son. The Deputy Principal did contact me 5 months later, again on behalf of the Principal, to say sorry for our loss, and asked to acknowledge Maddy's death in the school magazine. The Deputy Principal is a lovely lady, and I did appreciate the call. It did give me a chance to talk about the bullying that Maddy had to deal with at school, and the psychological trauma it left her with for the rest of her life. I did feel that this allowed me some closure for Maddy.

Maddy's high school did print something in their school magazine "Maddy Ryan" and dates. There was nothing written about Maddy at all; nothing about the contribution she made to the school or the beautiful person she was. In contrast, the school Maddy taught at put a half page article about her in their school magazine, and again on the anniversary of her death. It just shows how the actions and inactions of people can have an everlasting impact.

I now look back and feel honoured by the school Maddy taught at, and her primary school, that they cared so much for her. I look back now at Maddy's secondary school and hope that Maddy's story will help them to ensure better policies for dealing with bullying for their future students.

Many of the stories about Maddy gave me great comfort. I had a beautiful work associate of Maddy's come to our home with a gorgeous arrangement of flowers one day. This lady told me many stories about Maddy. How happy Maddy was with our new home, how much she loved us, speaking often about her brother and what he was up to. These stories were good to hear. She went on to say that Maddy's gift was her special connection to the children, particularly those with special needs. She said that children were drawn to her and she was their favourite among the staff.

The staff called Maddy the "whisperer" as she was the only one who could settle the children before their afternoon nap. Maddy was gentle and kind and the children responded to her because of those traits. This lady said that I never needed to worry that Maddy would not be a mother, she said "Maddy was a mother to hundreds of children". I had not looked at it like that, but her stories comforted me and will stay with me always.

I felt that I needed closure by meeting the children that Maddy had taught, and meeting the staff who were so special to her. I went with my sister one Friday morning. It was more emotional than I had expected, but very beneficial for all of us.

The staff came in at different times, some fighting back tears, we received many hugs. They were the most divine human beings, how lucky Maddy was to share her days with them. We sat and chatted after meeting the children, we heard many stories.

It was comforting to know how much Maddy talked of me, how much she loved me. One of the teaching staff said that she and Maddy were chatting one day about their mothers. This lady asked Maddy if she was close to her mother. Maddy told the lady that she adored me and I was her best friend. Hearing this was overwhelmingly emotional for me at the time. As Maddy had taken her own life, and I was the last person that I know of to speak to her, I was left with so much pain over our last conversation. To hear those words were the greatest comfort for me. I have been able to focus on those words, and remind myself that I tried so hard to be the best mother I could to her. As time has gone by, I feel more at peace because of that story. It is something I always remind myself of when the dark memories try to creep back.

I loved hearing about all the things she did that I had no idea about. One story was of an excursion with the children. Maddy noticed a bird trapped in some netting. Maddy raced over to the bird, crawled under the netting, all the children were apparently enthralled, watching her, she carefully removed the bird from the netting and set it free.

Another was of her talking to the chef at the school about food (of course there had to be a story about food). Maddy was preparing a recipe book containing some of my recipes, her partner's Mum's recipes and others that took her fancy. Apparently, she had asked the chef to teach her how to make roasted eggplant and panna cotta. The chef and Maddy arranged for Maddy to come in early one day and she would teach her how to make the recipes. Maddy died so they never got to do it. The teaching staff told me that a couple of weeks after Maddy died the chef made the roasted eggplant and panna cotta for the staff in memory of Maddy. I met the chef, she could not speak to me, her face said it all, her hug said it all – she truly loved my beautiful daughter.

Another story was from a work colleague who told me that she watched Maddy out of a window one day. Maddy was walking in the sunshine. The sun shone down on her long golden hair, Maddy was looking around at the scenery and up at the sky. This lady said how beautiful she looked. Maddy looked peaceful and happy. It reminded me of when she was little, looking up at the sky at the birds, chasing butterflies and chasing the blue balloon on her last day of primary school.

I have said on many occasions through this book that Maddy loved animals and nature. Maddy took care of the class pets at the school she worked at. The class pets were stick insects. These are awful looking bugs, in my opinion. I remember her bringing them home one school holidays and leaving them on our dining room table. I was horrified when I went into the room and she had them on her head and shoulders and arms. Maddy wanted me to hold them, I was completely freaked out. Maddy thought this was hilarious, she loved making fun of me. Sometimes I think it was her favourite pastime.

The teacher said to me that Maddy always cleaned the stick insect enclosure, fed them and took care of them. The teacher believed she really did love these bugs. I was told that in all the years that they had these bugs, they never bred. They never, ever had one baby bug, and they had these stick insects for as many years as she could remember.

The week Maddy died, one morning as the staff arrived they checked the enclosure and there were hundreds of baby stick insects. The staff were all crying, they believed it was a gift from Maddy.

Observe everything, never assume anything and go with the flow, whatever happens. This is what I have tried to do in my life, and so many things give me comfort now.

*Chapter 9*

# ADVOCATING FOR POSITIVE MENTAL HEALTH AWARENESS

**BREAKTHROUGH MENTAL HEALTH RESEARCH FOUNDATION REPORT:**

- Eight Australians die from suicide every day

- More young Australians aged 15 – 44, die from suicide than any other cause

- $60 billion is the annual cost of mental illness in Australia

- One in five Australians has a mental health issue

- 50% of diagnosable mental illness onsets between the ages of 11 and 14

- 75% of diagnosable mental illness onsets before the age of 24

For Maddy, her mental health presented at age 13 and she took her life at age 23.

What can we do to stop mental health trauma? I guess for many of us that question seems insurmountable. I personally believe that we need to start when children are young. We need to teach them positivity, self-love, resilience and the importance of healthy relationships. Kindness needs to be taught as part of wellbeing education.

If the community were to help carry the banner for mental health awareness by not being afraid to speak of their problems, to share with the ones that love them, not be judgmental, then perhaps we can move toward removing the stigma attached to mental health.

If those that witness inappropriate behaviour report these issues, so that action can be taken to help victims then we could encourage behaviour of reporting and supporting. If these things were to happen, then I feel it would be a great leap forward for positive mental health in our community.

We need to teach them positivity, self-love, resilience and the importance of healthy relationships.

*Chapter 11*

# RECOVERY

**I WAS DETERMINED** that Maddy's death would not define me or my future. I refused to walk around with a dark cloud over me, I did not want pity over the tragedy that had struck my life. From my perspective, there was nothing to pity, people lose loved ones every day and I was just one of those people, it is part of life. Certainly, the loss of our daughter was horrific, but I think there are people much worse off than me. My husband had a heart attack 8 weeks after Maddy died. The medical staff said it was from stress. I needed to be the strong one for my husband and my son and I was going to show them that we all had a right to our own life, a happy life, it would just be a different life without Maddy in it.

Maddy was gone, I made peace with that. I would tell her story, advocate for mental health awareness in her memory, and I would have a joyful and fulfilling life. For me, this has become about helping others. I have great pleasure from helping those who reach out to me, and I enjoy the connections I have made through becoming involved in charity work.

I can honestly say at this point in my life, that I have found a place of acceptance, peace and happiness. I miss my girl every day. However, I continue to be grateful for having her in my life, for the joy she brought me and for the things that she taught me. I count my blessings daily – my dedicated husband, amazing son, wonderful family and friends, my gaggle of Pugs, my beautiful home and my health. I live in a vibrant seaside village where I also get a lot of support from neighbours and local business, I am surrounded by kind people. I could not ask for anything more.

I sometimes wondered during my recovery whether I had bad karma, that my beautiful, golden haired child could be ripped from my life in such tragic circumstances. The truth is I received my karma in the amount of people that came to me to carry me through. I remain the most blessed and lucky person to have so much love in my life.

I have also wondered whether cause and effect would catch up with the bullies that impacted so heavily on Maddy's life. I do not wish them any harm, I feel only pity for them. They will always live with the knowledge of how cruel they were to Maddy, and the part they played in her life. The people that bullied Maddy, and also those who were unkind to her during her life; they were not responsible for Maddy's death. However, they did impact on who she became in life, her perfectionist behaviour, her fear of rejection, her anxiety and her insecurities. Those people were the catalyst for what became Maddy's mental health issues.

I think Maddy's experiences made her super kind. I believe she purposely tried to live a good and productive life. I believe that Maddy's final decision was a mistake, a spur of the moment decision to end her pain, that on any given day, and under different circumstances that she would never have wanted to take her own life.

In the weeks after Maddy died, we received a lot of shopping that she had done on line. The shopping amounted to hundreds of dollars. Packages were sent to our house and to her partner's house. Maddy had made dates with girlfriends to catch up, she had plans. It is done though, she has gone, and now the rest of us are left to go on with life without her beauty and kindness in it. I often think that perhaps some souls are just too special, too sensitive, too kind to live in this harsh world.

I have researched much about mental health issues over the years. People say you should never Google symptoms and self-diagnose, but I do believe Maddy suffered from Post-Traumatic Stress Disorder. It was never diagnosed professionally, but the symptoms appear parallel to what Maddy suffered.

The following information is from the Black Dog Institute describing Post-Traumatic Stress Disorder. *"We have strong reactions to traumatic events – at times in our lives we may encounter traumatic experiences that threaten the life or safety of ourselves or others. Most of us will have a strong reaction to these extreme and distressing events.*

*Feelings of fear, sadness, anger and grief are common after a traumatic event. This is part of our natural human response. Over time, with support from family and friends, we start to make sense of what's happened. These feelings usually fade and we recover. However, sometimes witnessing a distressing event can lead to severe feelings of fear and anguish that stay with us for a long time. These feelings start to interfere with our lives and stop us doing what we used to do. When this happens, we need to get help to get through it."*

*Seek professional help. There are always people who can help you.*

The only way schools will ever stop bullying is to have ongoing, evidence-based healthy relationship programs in place. Look at policies and procedures, put checklists in place so everybody knows the quickest and most effective course of action. Reports, innuendo, hearsay – it should all be investigated.

From my own experiences, I can only offer this advice - for those with mental health issues, seek professional help. There are always people who can help you, just reach out. Call Lifeline, Beyond Blue, Kids Helpline or any organisation that gives such support. Seek out professional help with a medical professional that you have faith in. Talk to friends or family, talking helps. Always remember how special you are.

For those who are supporting those who are being bullied or those with mental health issues - always be available to talk, try to keep calm, look after yourself and seek professional advice whenever you need to. Keep bullying out in the open, do not cover it up, do not ignore it. If it is a child who is being bullied, speak to the school and ask to see their policies to ensure that you know the processes to follow. Work together with the school. If you are not getting the support you need from the school hierarchy, go to the school board, go to your local government member, go to whomever you need to get action to help you. Never underestimate the effect bullying has on the individual.

To those of you that bully, please stop. Please remember Maddy every time you are mean to another person. Ask yourself, do I really want to cause this pain to another person, another family, another community? Remember Maddy's struggles, remember me, remember how much I loved her and how much I miss her. Please remember our story.

I continue to get comfort from the impact Maddy made on the lives of others. I have learned many things about Maddy since she died; things that I would not have ordinarily known. I know her life made a difference. I raised a beautiful, kind human being. Maddy made a lasting imprint on those that were blessed with loving her and knowing her. I remain astonished at the extent of her social network and the amount of people who quite obviously adored her. Many people could live a life time and never make the impact that Maddy made on the lives of others in her 23 years.

If we can have so many people love us at the end of our life, isn't that something we should all aspire to?

Maddy's death does not define her life. Maddy fought to live a good life. I believe she tried hard - her life was so special, she was special, I remain the proudest mum to the most beautiful girl.

We all have a beginning and an end, it is how we fill the in between (our dash) that matters. Maddy's dash was shorter than some, but her dash was extraordinary, she was extraordinary, she was mine, I love her and I miss her.

### *How Do You Live Your Dash?*

*I read of a man who stood to speak*
*At the funeral of a friend.*
*He referred to the dates on her tombstone*
*From the beginning to the end*
*He noted he first came to her date of birth*
*And spoke the following date with tears,*
*But he said what mattered most of all*
*Was the dash between those years. (1900 – 1970)*

*For that dash represents all the time*
*That she spent alive on this earth…*
*And now only those who loved her*
*Know what that little line is worth.*
*For it matters not, how much we own:*
*The cars…the house…the cash,*
*What matters is how we live and love*
*And how we spend our dash.*

*So think about this long and hard….*
*Are there things you'd like to change?*
*For you never know how much time is left*
*That can still be rearranged.*
*If we could just slow down enough*
*To consider what's true and real,*
*And always try to understand*
*The way other people feel.*

*And be less quick to anger*
*And show appreciation more*
*And love the people in our lives*
*Like we've never loved before.*
*If we treat each other with respect,*
*And more often wear a smile….*
*Remembering that this special dash*
*Might only last a little while.*

*So when your eulogy's being read*
*With your life's actions to rehash*
*Would you be proud of the things they say*
*About how you spent your dash?*

*(by Linda Ellis)*

**IN LOVING MEMORY** of our daughter
**MADELEINE PAIGE RYAN**
**1995 - 2018**

# RESOURCES

| | |
|---|---|
| **BEYOND BLUE** | 1300 22 4636 |
| **LIFELINE** | 13 11 14 |
| **KIDS HELP LINE** | 1800 551 800 |